Discover & Learn

Vikings

Years 5-6

This Teacher Book is the perfect companion to CGP's 'Vikings' Activity Book for Years 5-6.

It contains a range of useful resources, including answers, information for teachers, prompts and guidance for pupils, and suggestions for extension activities.

It's ideal for helping your pupils explore the KS2 History topic 'The Viking and Anglo-Saxon struggle for the Kingdom of England to the time of Edward the Confessor'.

Who Were The Vikings?

Vikings: Activity Book p.2-3

2

Who Were The Vikings?

The Vikings came from several <u>countries</u>.

The map below shows the countries they were from, and some of the countries they travelled to for raids.

Look at the map. Colour the countries the Vikings came from in <u>red</u>.

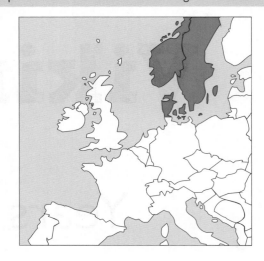

Read pages 2 and 3 of your Study Book.

Complete the sentences below. You might want to use the <u>key words</u> in the box to help you write the sentences.

Key Words
| slaves | fame | ships | money | treasure |

Vikings travelled _across the sea in ships._

Vikings raided because _they wanted to make money and find fame. They did this by stealing treasure and taking people to use as slaves._

Extension Idea

As well as Britain, the Vikings raided Ireland, France, Finland, Spain and Italy. Pupils could find these countries on a <u>map</u>, then colour and label them here.

Extension Idea

Pupils could investigate the countries further afield which the Vikings reached (e.g. Russia and Turkey).

More able pupils may mention that the ships were called <u>longships</u>.

Extension Idea

Ask pupils to imagine meeting a Viking for the first time. What would they notice? What would they think of them? Ask pupils to write a diary entry about the meeting.

Who Were The Vikings?: National Curriculum Aims

- Know and understand the history of Britain as a chronological narrative.
- Know about the history of the wider world.
- Create structured accounts.

The weather tended to be warmer in Britain than in the Viking countries.

Why might <u>warmer weather</u> in Britain have made the Vikings want to settle there?

A warmer climate may have encouraged the Vikings to settle in Britain because _it might have made it easier to farm. Crops would have grown better there than in the colder Viking countries. It might also have been more pleasant to live in a warmer place._

Pupil Guidance:

"Think about how the warmer weather could have affected the Vikings' <u>food supply</u>."

Imagine that you are a Viking who is <u>visiting England</u>. Write a letter to your brother, Ulfketyl, <u>describing</u> England and explaining <u>why</u> he might like to travel to England too.

Suggested Scaffolding:

"Try and include these words in your answer:
- farm
- crops"

Dear Ulfketyl,

Greetings from England! _The journey across the sea was quite calm and we had no problems. I really think you'd like England, so you should come on the next raiding trip. It's much warmer here than back home in Norway. There's also fertile land, and the people here are growing lots of crops. They will have a lot of food to harvest this year because of the good weather. We did some raiding when we arrived, so we've got lots of treasure to bring home. See you soon!_

Suggested Scaffolding:

"Try and include these words in your answer:
- weather
- land
- raids / raiding"

Pupils could talk about the <u>differences</u> between Scandinavia and England that would have made <u>England</u> seem more <u>attractive</u> to the Vikings.

"I understand who the Vikings were and why they raided Britain."

Extension Idea

Pupils could sign off with a Viking name. For this they could do some internet research into Old Norse names and what they mean. For example, the girl's name Gudrun means 'god's secret lore', and the boy's name Siegfried means 'victory-peace'.

Vikings: Activity Book p.4-5

4

Viking Values

Anglo-Saxons and Vikings spoke different <u>languages</u>.
Anglo-Saxons in England spoke <u>Old English</u>. Some Vikings spoke <u>Old Icelandic</u>.
There were some <u>similarities</u> between these languages.

On the left are some Old English words. On the right are some Old Icelandic words. Draw lines to join up each Old English word with the Old Icelandic word you think <u>sounds</u> or <u>looks</u> most <u>similar</u>. One has been done for you.

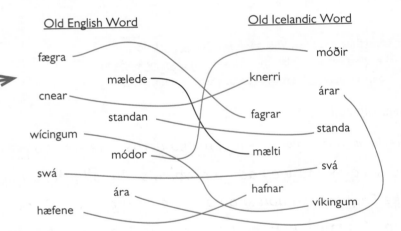

Use pages 4 and 5 of the Study Book to find out if these sentences about Vikings are <u>true</u> or <u>false</u>. Tick the correct box for each statement.

The Vikings followed a Pagan religion.   True ✓ False ☐

The Vikings raided Lindisfarne priory in AD 693.   True ☐ False ✓

The Anglo-Saxons in Britain had originally
followed a Pagan religion.   True ✓ False ☐

The Vikings arrived at Lindisfarne by boat.   True ✓ False ☐

The Havamal was a Viking god.   True ☐ False ✓

Suggested Scaffolding:

"Here are some more pairs to help you:
- cnear — knerri
- fægra — fagrar"

Meanings of the Old English words in modern English:
- fægra — good
- mælede — counselled
- cnear — ship
- standan — standing
- wícingum — to go pirating
- módor — mother
- swá — course
- ára — oars
- hæfene — haven

Extension Idea

Ask pupils to suggest reasons <u>why</u> there are <u>similar words</u> in the two languages.

Here is a Modern English translation of the poem in the Study Book:

Thus counselled my mother
For me should they purchase
A galley and good oars
To go forth a-viking
So may I high-standing
A noble ship steering
Hold course for the haven
Hew down many foemen.

Extension Idea

More able pupils could be asked to give a <u>correct version</u> of the false statements.

Viking Values: National Curriculum Aims

- Know about the history of the wider world.
- Understand similarity and difference and use them to draw contrasts.
- Create structured accounts.

5

Vikings wrote stories about their voyages on <u>runestones</u>.
Lots of runestones can still be seen today in the countries where the Vikings came from. This picture shows a runestone in Sweden.

Imagine you've been on a Viking voyage to raid England. Write a short story about your trip that could be written on a runestone.

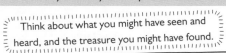
Think about what you might have seen and heard, and the treasure you might have found.

We reached the shore of England just after dawn. We could see a monastery on a hill, so we headed quickly towards that. Suddenly, shouting broke the peaceful silence — the monks must have seen us coming. We raided the monastery, and took home lots of glittering treasures.

Vikings were expected to behave in certain ways.

Read page 5 of the Study Book, then write down <u>two</u> 'Viking rules' about how to behave.

Rule 1 *Always be honourable / truthful / brave.*

....

Rule 2 *Have good manners.*

....

"I know about Viking writing and language, and about how Vikings were expected to behave."

Well-known Viking runestones include the <u>Jelling Stones</u> found in Denmark.

A wide range of answers are possible, but they should all fit in with what pupils know about Viking raids. Higher ability pupils should try to make their stories <u>interesting</u> by varying their sentence structures.

Extension Idea

Pupils could be given a copy of a Viking <u>runic alphabet</u> from the internet. They could have a go at writing a short <u>inscription</u> to go on a runestone using the runic letters.

Extension Idea

Pupils could discuss how we know how to behave today. How similar are the Viking rules about how to behave to our <u>own rules</u>? Or to <u>school rules</u>?

Norse Beliefs

Vikings: Activity Book p.6-7

Pupils may be familiar with some of the names of the Norse gods (e.g. Thor, Odin and Loki), and some of the places (e.g. Bifrost and Asgard) from recent <u>films</u> and <u>comics</u>.

Extension Idea

Pupils could write some <u>new</u> true or false questions using the information on pages 6 and 7 of the Study Book and then swap their questions with a partner.

Suggested Scaffolding:

Pupils could be given the words needed to complete the sentences in a jumbled up order.

Extension Idea

Pupils could make a card matching game. The <u>names</u> of the gods and goddesses are listed on one set of cards, and their <u>roles</u> are listed on another set. These are then all turned <u>face down</u>, and pupils take turns to turn over one of each type of card, until all the pairs have been correctly matched up.

6

Norse Beliefs

Viking religion involved several worlds and several gods. They also believed in an afterlife — but which afterlife you went to depended on how you had behaved in life.

Use pages 6 and 7 of the Study Book to find out if these sentences about Viking beliefs are <u>true</u> or <u>false</u>. Tick the correct box for each statement.

The Vikings believed there was more than one world. — True ✓ False ☐

The Vikings believed that humans lived in a world called Asgard. — True ☐ False ✓

The Vikings believed that humans could live in different worlds. — True ☐ False ✓

The father of the Viking gods was Thor. — True ☐ False ✓

The Vikings believed a bridge called Bifrost linked Asgard and Midgard. — True ✓ False ☐

Use page 7 of the Study Book to help you complete the sentences below.

Thor was the god of <u>thunder.</u>

Odin's wife was called <u>Frigg.</u>

Tyr was the god of <u>war and justice.</u>

Odin ruled <u>Valhalla.</u>

Make up a Viking god or goddess of your own, and give him or her a name. What would they be a god or goddess of?

Name <u>Scavellyn</u>

God/Goddess of <u>mountains</u>

Extension Idea

Pupils could <u>research</u> other Norse gods and goddesses, and record what they were gods and goddesses of.

Norse Beliefs: National Curriculum Aims

- Know about the history of the wider world.
- Understand the connections between religious and social history.
- Create structured accounts.

Vikings believed that if they died bravely in battle, they would be taken to <u>Valhalla</u> in the afterlife.

Imagine you are a Viking. Write down <u>why</u> you want to go to Valhalla.

I want to go to Valhalla in the afterlife because there are feasts every day, and the food and drink never run out. I would be treated like a hero.

Pupil Guidance:

"Think about how the Vikings thought they'd be <u>treated</u> there."

Draw what you imagine Valhalla might look like.
Add some labels to explain what is happening in your picture.

Pupils should show that it would be a <u>good place</u> to be, e.g. by showing the Vikings as being happy. They could show the Vikings eating and drinking at a feast.

Pupil Guidance:

"Think about how the people there would be <u>feeling</u>, and what they would be <u>doing</u>."

Extension Idea

Valhalla was an endless round of feasting, drinking and fighting, just what Norse warriors loved. Pupils could investigate how different religions have different afterlives, and whether these reflect what the religion values.

"I know about Viking gods and goddesses, and what the Vikings believed about the afterlife."

Extension Idea

Thor, Tyr, and Loki often went out on adventures together. These usually went well... unless Loki was in a mischievous mood and decided to double-cross his fellow gods! Pupils could read some Norse myths, and create their own story using some of the gods and goddesses as characters.

Viking Voyages

Vikings: Activity Book p.8-9

8

Viking Voyages

Archaeology has allowed us to find out lots about where the Vikings went.
Read pages 8 and 9 of the Study Book.

What sorts of things have <u>archaeologists</u> found
that can tell us where Vikings travelled to?

Archaeologists have found *items in Viking hoards that have*
come from different countries. For example, they have
found foreign coins.

Imagine <u>you</u> went on holiday to a <u>different country</u> today.
What <u>evidence</u> might archaeologists find in the <u>future</u> to show that
you had travelled there? Write or draw your answer in the box.

We know that some Vikings made it as far as <u>Canada</u>.

List some <u>other countries</u> that we know that Vikings travelled to.

England, Scotland, Ireland, Russia, Syria, Iraq

Extension Idea

Pupils could discuss whether these finds <u>definitely prove</u> that the Vikings travelled to foreign countries. They could be asked to give <u>other reasons</u> for why they've been found in Viking hoards, e.g. foreign travellers coming to Scandinavia and trading the items there.

A variety of answers is possible here. Pupils could list or draw <u>souvenirs</u>, <u>postcards</u> with foreign stamps, <u>passport stamps</u>, or boat, train and plane <u>tickets</u> and <u>boarding passes</u>.

Pupil Guidance:

"Think about the sorts of things you might bring back from holiday as <u>souvenirs</u> or <u>presents</u>. Would there be any written evidence of your trip?"

The Vikings also travelled to countries in northern, central and southern Europe.

Viking Voyages: National Curriculum Aims

- Know about the history of the wider world.
- Understand how evidence is used to make historical claims.
- Create structured accounts.

9

How can we tell that Vikings actually <u>settled</u> in Canada rather than just raiding?

> Remember, if the Vikings were just raiding, they wouldn't have stayed long.

We can tell that Vikings settled in Canada because the remains of a settlement have been found on a site in Canada. Archaeologists have found items like pins, knitting needles and spindles there, which suggests women travelled there too.

Higher ability pupils may write that this settlement is called <u>l'Anse aux Meadows</u> and is in Newfoundland, Canada.

Extension Idea

Some archaeologists think that the Vikings only stayed at l'Anse aux Meadows for a <u>few years</u>. Can you suggest why they left again?

Imagine you're a Viking travelling from Norway to Canada. Write a short story about your <u>journey</u>. Write about how you would have travelled, and what the difficulties would have been.

> You can use page 9 of the Study Book for help.

I set off with the rest of the Viking crew on a long journey by ship. It was pretty tough. The weather was stormy and the seas were very rough. I felt quite seasick! It took us a long time — we were nearly running out of food by the time we got to North America. We found our way there using the Sun and stars to guide us but, because of the rough weather, we nearly got lost once or twice. The journey was very tiring — I'm not sure I want to go again in a hurry!

Pupil Guidance:

"Think about how <u>long</u> your journey would have been. What would the ship have been like to travel on?"

Suggested Scaffolding:

- 'We travelled by...'
- 'The weather was...'
- 'Our food was...'
- 'We found our way by...'

"I know where the Vikings travelled to and how they travelled."

Extension Idea

Research the city of Constantinople, where there were Viking guards in the Byzantine Emperor's palace (the Varangian Guard) from the 9th century. What would a Viking find amazing about this city? Pupils could write a letter home from a Viking guard, describing the city and life there.

Raiding and Trading

Vikings: Activity Book p.10-11

Vikings had an almost romantic relationship with the sea, for which they had kennings such as 'swans' road' or 'whales' way'. They were not sentimental about it however, and they understood its dangers. Ran was the goddess of the sea, and the sea is sometimes referred to as 'Ran's mouth'. To die at sea was to 'lie in Ran's bed' — many Vikings ended life there. Jormungand, the Midgard Serpent, was thought to encircle the sea with his huge body and tail. When he thrashed around, it would cause storms which would wreck many knarrs (boats).

10

Raiding and Trading

Vikings were experts at <u>boat building</u> and <u>sea travel</u>.

Archaeologists have discovered some well-preserved Viking longships.

This picture shows what a Viking longship might have looked like.

Read page 10 of the Study Book. Write down <u>two materials</u> that would have been used to make a Viking longship.

Material 1) _wood_   Material 2) _iron_

Use the <u>picture above</u> and page 10 of the Study Book to draw a picture of a Viking longship. <u>Label</u> and <u>explain</u> the features that make the ship suited to raiding voyages.

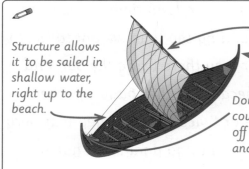

A sail, to help the ship travel quickly, using the wind.

Structure allows it to be sailed in shallow water, right up to the beach.

Double-ended, so it could be pushed quickly off the beach backwards and rowed away to sea.

Would <u>you</u> have wanted to travel across the sea in a longship? Why, or why not?

....

....

Extension Idea

Pupils could be asked to imagine that they are Vikings who are <u>upgrading</u> their boats. They should come up with some extra design features for the boats which would make the sea journeys more comfortable.

Pupils can either say that they would or they wouldn't want to travel in a longship, as long as they support their decision with a good reason.

Raiding and Trading: National Curriculum Aims

- Know about the history of the wider world.
- Create structured accounts.

11

The Vikings carried out a lot of trading. One thing they traded was <u>slaves</u>.

Use page 11 of the Study Book to find out if these sentences about slavery during Viking times are <u>true</u> or <u>false</u>. Tick the correct box for each statement.

Slavery was allowed in Europe during the Viking times. True ✓ False ☐

The Vikings would always buy their slaves. True ☐ False ✓

Vikings would sell slaves in markets in other countries. True ✓ False ☐

Slaves were used by the Vikings as farm workers. True ✓ False ☐

If you had lived in the Viking times, would you have <u>agreed</u> with slavery? Why, or why not?

....

....

....

The Vikings didn't just trade slaves.

Draw a <u>circle</u> around each of the <u>two</u> sentences below that you think are <u>correct</u>. Use page 11 of the Study Book if you need help.

The Vikings couldn't get amber or animal furs from Scandinavia, so they bought them.

The Vikings bought everything they needed.

The Vikings traded with ivory from Scandinavia.

The Vikings often traded for silver and gold.

"I know about how Vikings travelled and how they traded slaves and goods."

Extension Idea

Pupils could do their own research into slavery in order to find out when it was <u>abolished</u> in European countries.

Although it has been abolished officially, does slavery still exist in the modern world? Investigate and discuss.

Suggested Scaffolding:

'I would / wouldn't have agreed with slavery because...'

Extension Idea

Pupils could be asked to write two more <u>true</u> <u>sentences</u> about Viking trading. They can use page 11 of the Study Book to help them.

Extension Idea

Pupils could investigate the Gokstad ship, and how a replica was made and sailed across the Atlantic. They could investigate what food would last on the journey, and how people would find fresh water to drink. Pupils could present their findings as a fact file on Viking Voyages.

Viking Visits

Vikings: Activity Book p.12-13

It is impossible to know exactly why the raid on Lindisfarne took place, and why the Vikings had decided to turn their attention to England. A clue may exist in the Anglo-Saxon Chronicle for 793 AD which says that after frightening omens of lightning and dragons flying through the air, there was 'a great famine'. If there was a famine in Scandinavia as well, this would provide a reason for the raid, since the Norsemen would be looking for people and goods to trade for food for their own survival.

Extension Idea
Higher ability pupils could write out <u>correct versions</u> of the incorrect sentences.

Pupils' answers will vary. Most pupils will probably write that they would feel scared because the Vikings are likely to hurt them and the other monks.

12

Viking Visits

A lot of Viking raids happened in Britain — Scandinavia was so close that the Vikings were able to reach Britain by boat within a <u>few days</u>, if the weather was good.

Use pages 12 and 13 of the Study Book to find out if these sentences about Viking visits are <u>true</u> or <u>false</u>. Tick the correct box for each statement.

The Vikings first visited England in about AD 787.   True ✓ False ☐

The Vikings' first visit to England was to Lindisfarne.   True ☐ False ✓

The Vikings often raided places on the British coast.   True ✓ False ☐

The Vikings settled in Lindisfarne.   True ☐ False ✓

Lindisfarne was near lots of other towns.   True ☐ False ✓

The Vikings took some of the monks from Lindisfarne priory as slaves.   True ✓ False ☐

Some people thought that the Viking raids were a punishment from God for sinning.   True ✓ False ☐

The first Viking raid in England was on the <u>priory</u> on the island of <u>Lindisfarne</u>.

Read page 13 of the Study Book and have a look at the picture. Imagine that you are a <u>monk</u> living in Lindisfarne priory during the first Viking raid. In the speech bubble below, write down how you think you would <u>feel</u> and <u>why</u>.

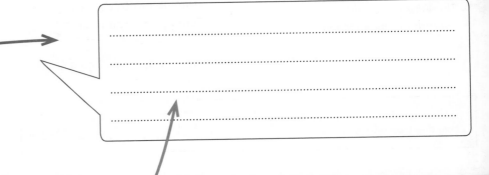

Extension Idea
Pupils could plan and perform a television news item about the Lindisfarne attack, as if they were a reporter covering the story. Their broadcast should contain eye-witness accounts, and a comment on the situation from a local king or thegn.

Viking Visits: National Curriculum Aims

- Know and understand the history of Britain as a chronological narrative.
- Create structured accounts.
- Know how Britain has been influenced by the wider world.

The Vikings <u>stole</u> lots of things during their raid of Lindisfarne.

Draw a picture of <u>two</u> things that the Vikings might have stolen during their raid on Lindisfarne. Use page 12 of the Study Book to help you.

The pupils can draw any two of the things listed on page 12 of the Study Book. For example, silver treasures, plates, candlesticks and books.

Extension Idea

Pupils could imagine that the Vikings have raided their <u>school</u> or <u>home</u> today. They could write a <u>newspaper article</u> describing what happened and what the Vikings stole.

Imagine you are a <u>Viking</u> who took part in the raid on Lindisfarne. Describe what you would have <u>seen</u> and how you might have <u>felt</u> when you arrived on the shore.

I saw the priory in the distance and some people on the shore looking out to sea at us. I didn't know whether they would fight us, but I was feeling brave. I was also excited about the treasures we might find, and I hoped I'd be able to take home some slaves to work on my land.

Suggested Scaffolding:

- 'I saw the priory and...'
- 'The monks looked...'
- 'I felt...'

"I know about the first Viking raid on England."

Extension Idea

Many historic events of this time were written down as songs or poems. Pupils could write a song or poem detailing the events of the Lindisfarne raid, from either the Vikings' or monks' perspective.

Violent Vikings?

Vikings: Activity Book p.14-15

Violent Vikings?

From what we know about the Vikings, it seems like they lived in a <u>violent society</u>.

The <u>Anglo-Saxons</u> wrote about the Viking raids. Can you think of any reasons why they might have made the Vikings seem <u>more violent</u> than they actually were?

> The Anglo-Saxons were the people living in England at the time of the Viking raids.

The Anglo-Saxons might have made the Vikings seem more violent because they might have been shocked that they would attack the Christian church and might have wanted to give the Vikings a bad name.

Many of the Viking attacks were written about by monks. As <u>victims</u> of the attacks, the monks obviously weren't too keen to write nice things about the Vikings!

Read page 14 of the Study Book. What <u>evidence</u> is there in the Norse language that suggests the Vikings lived in a violent society?

The sagas are stories written in the Norse language. They include descriptions of Viking violence. For example, in Njal's Saga, one killing leads to another, then another.

Pupils may also write about <u>weapons</u> being described in sagas.

The Vikings developed a <u>justice system</u>. You can read about it on page 15 of the Study Book.

One of the punishments in the Viking justice system was paying '<u>wergild</u>'. In your own words, write down what paying wergild meant.

If somebody was killed, their family would be paid wergild by the killer. This was money to compensate for their death.

Extension Idea

Pupils could find out more about Njal's Saga online. Some people believe that the sagas were actually written to warn people of the awful consequences of blood feuds, not to celebrate Viking brutality. Ask pupils what they think about this. Discuss, and come to a conclusion.

Extension Idea

Pupils could be asked to consider whether they think the <u>family</u> would feel that the wergild made up for their relative's death.

Violent Vikings?: National Curriculum Aims

- Understand how evidence is used to make historical claims.
- Understand change.
- Understand the connections between social and political history.

15

Apart from paying wergild, write down two other punishments from the Viking justice system.

Punishment 1 _Fines_

Punishment 2 _Outlawing_

What punishments are there for criminals in Britain today? Write down any that you know about in the box below.

> ✎ _E.g. prison, fines, electronic tagging, community service_

Other answers are possible here. Pupils may try to describe punishments they don't know the name of, for example, writing 'clean up rubbish' instead of 'community service'.

A group of Vikings moved to Iceland and settled there in around AD 870. Some years later, they set up a government there.

Use page 15 of the Study Book to find out if these sentences are true or false. Tick the correct box for each statement.

Statement	True	False
The Vikings set up their government in Iceland at a place called Althing.		✓
The law-speaker had to learn all of the Viking laws.	✓	
The Viking laws were always written down.		✓
All Viking crimes had the same punishment.		✓
The law-speaker would stand on Thingvellir Rock to speak.		✓

Extension Idea

Think about why the Vikings might have set up a government — why might it have been needed, and what would it have helped with?

"I know about violence, justice and punishment in Viking society."

👍 ✓ 👎 ✓ 👎 ✓

Extension Idea

The Althing is considered to be the oldest parliament in the world, and Icelanders are very proud of it. Pupils could research it further, and create a poster to celebrate it.

16

More Viking Visits

Vikings: Activity Book p.16-17

Ireland also suffered many Viking raids. From 800 to 830, the Irish Annals record that the Vikings raided the coasts of Ireland over 25 times, working from their Scottish bases. By 837 the Vikings had established camp at Dublin, and by 842 they were staying there over the winter.

Suggested Scaffolding:

"Try to include these words in your answer:

- *land*
- *Norway*
- *Britain*
- *raids"*

Pupils may give a variety of answers here, but they must be related to the picture in the Study Book.

16

More Viking Visits

Some of the first Vikings that settled in Britain settled on the Scottish island of Orkney.

Read page 16 of the Study Book. Now imagine you are a Viking who has just settled on Orkney. Write a letter to your friend Hrolf telling him why Orkney is such a great place to be and why he should come over to Orkney too.

Dear Hrolf,

Orkney is such a great place! There's so much space here. My family have built a house, and we have plenty of land to grow crops on. You and your family should consider joining us — there is still some free land that you could have. It only took us two days to sail here, so it's easy to get back to Norway if we need to. Also, we're in a great position to go on raids to the rest of Britain — it doesn't take long to go south along the coast to find the treasure!

Imagine you are one of the people in the painting on page 17 of the Study Book. You are in England waiting for the Viking ships to arrive. Write down:

One thing you can see: ....

One thing you can hear: ....

One thing you might say to the people standing next to you: ....

Extension Idea

Pupils could investigate the history of Norse occupation of Orkney and the Shetlands, and discover the Norse words that have survived to this day in the Orcadian and Shetlandic dialects.

More Viking Visits: National Curriculum Aims

- Know and understand the history of Britain as a chronological narrative.
- Create structured accounts.
- Understand connections between local and national history.

Look at this map of Britain. Some of the places <u>raided</u> by the Vikings are marked on it.

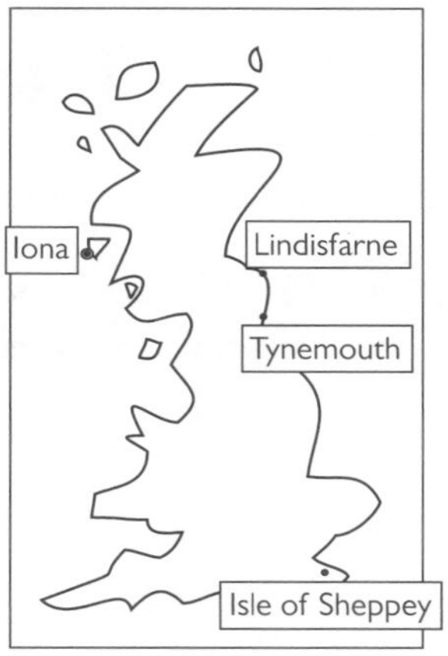

| What do all these places have in common? | Think about where all the places are. |

They're all around the coast of Britain.

Map labels: Iona, Lindisfarne, Tynemouth, Isle of Sheppey

Extension Idea

Pupils could be asked to discuss <u>why</u> the Vikings might have raided these places in particular, rather than any others.

In what part of Britain would you have felt safest living during the Viking attacks? Explain your answer.

I would have felt safest living in the middle of Britain, far away from the coast because the Vikings arrived by sea and raided places on the coast, so I'd be far away from them.

Pupil Guidance:

"Which would be the hardest places for the Vikings to get to?"

Read page 17 of the Study Book. In your own words, explain why the people of <u>Cornwall</u> might have had a good relationship with the Vikings.

The people of Cornwall mined tin. This was something that the Vikings might have wanted to trade for, so it was a good idea for the Vikings to have a good relationship with the people in Cornwall.

Suggested Scaffolding:

'The people of Cornwall mined...'

Pupils may also write about the Cornish <u>helping</u> the Vikings to <u>fight</u> the Anglo-Saxons. (Cornwall was populated by Celtic people who may have needed to defend themselves against the neighbouring Anglo-Saxon kingdom of Wessex.)

"I understand what effect repeated Viking raids had on people living in England."

Extension Idea

Pupils could be encouraged to discuss whether they think the people of Cornwall worried about the Vikings at all.

Viking Victories

Vikings: Activity Book p.18-19

18

Viking Victories

The Vikings kept on attacking the English coast. And they were starting to win...

Read page 18 of the Study Book. In AD 850, the Vikings spent the winter in England for the first time rather than going back to Scandinavia. What does this suggest?

It suggests that the Vikings were getting stronger, and were able to fight off the Anglo-Saxons.

The Vikings didn't try to fight the Anglo-Saxons during the winter. Why do you think the Vikings didn't want to fight in the winter?

It would have been cold, and there might not have been much food.

According to legend, <u>Ragnar Hairy Trousers</u> was a great Viking leader, whose death in England was responsible for the Great Heathen Army's attack on Britain.

Make up a story about how Ragnar Hairy Trousers got his <u>name</u>. Write down your story or draw what happens in the box below.

Pupil Guidance:

"What effects might the winter weather have had?"

There's no right answer here — the real reason for how Ragnar Hairy Trousers got his name isn't known. Some historians think that it was because he favoured trousers made from <u>animal skin</u>.

Extension Idea

Pupils could be asked to come up with a <u>Viking name</u> for themselves, and explain the reason behind their name.

Viking Victories: National Curriculum Aims

- Know and understand the history of Britain as a chronological narrative.
- Create structured accounts.

19

The Great Heathen Army invaded England in AD 865. This map shows the <u>kingdoms</u> in England at the time.

Using page 19 of the Study Book, find out which kingdom the Great Heathen Army first set up camp in. <u>Colour it in</u> on the map and <u>label it</u>.

Draw an <u>arrow</u> on the map to show the direction the Vikings went next.

East Anglia

In your own words, write down why the Anglo-Saxons couldn't stop these Viking invaders.

England at the time was split into several Anglo-Saxon kingdoms, which often argued. When the Vikings arrived, the Anglo-Saxons were too disorganised to fight together against them.

Imagine you are a solider in an Anglo-Saxon <u>fyrd</u>. The fyrd has been sent to fight the Great Heathen Army. Using everything you've learnt from pages 18 to 19 of the Study Book, write down how you feel about this and why.

....

....

....

....

"I know what happened when the Great Heathen Army attacked England."

The word 'fyrd' can either be pronounced 'feared', or to rhyme with 'bird'.

Pupils should have drawn an arrow pointing upwards/north from East Anglia.

Extension Idea

Pupils could do a <u>role-play</u>, where different people represent different kingdoms. They could have a <u>meeting</u> to discuss organising an <u>attack</u> against the Vikings.

Pupil Guidance:

"Think about how the fyrd had been gathered together — would it be a strong army?"

Pupils are likely to write that they would feel scared because there aren't enough men in the fyrd. The best answers should be linked to a specific pro/con of a fyrd.

Extension Idea

Pupils could research the British Army and the Royal Navy that we have today. If a similar system had been in place in 800 AD, do they think that the Vikings would have been able to take over so easily? Make sure pupils back up their answers with reasons.

Defeating the Anglo-Saxons

Vikings: Activity Book p.20-21

20

Defeating the Anglo-Saxons

Between 866 and 878, the Vikings slowly conquered most of the Anglo-Saxon kingdoms.

The timeline below shows some important events that took place in Britain between 866 and 878. Use pages 20 to 21 of the Study Book to fill in the gaps in the timeline.

Pupils might also write
Eoforwic — York's
Anglo-Saxon name.

AD 866 — The Vikings capture _York._

They rename it _Jorvik._

Extension Idea

Pupils could be asked to suggest _why_ the Vikings gave York a new name.

AD 867 — The Northumbrian kings, Aelle and Osbert are killed.

AD 870 — The Vikings return to _East Anglia._

They kill King _Edmund._

Pupils might also write that Alfred managed to keep the peace for 5 years.

AD 871 — _Alfred_ becomes king of Wessex.

He manages to _pay off the Vikings._

AD 876 — Guthrum, the new leader of the Danish Vikings, attacks Wessex.

Extension Idea

Pupils could discuss what the Vikings might have thought when Alfred retreated to Somerset.

AD 878 — _The Vikings attack Alfred at Chippenham and kill many of his men. Alfred runs away to Somerset._

Extension Idea

Pupils could create their own, longer timeline of events involving the Vikings in Britain, starting with the Vikings' first raid on Lindisfarne in AD 793.

Defeating the Anglo-Saxons: National Curriculum Aims

- Know and understand the history of Britain as a chronological narrative.
- Create structured accounts.
- Understand cause and consequence.

Each Anglo-Saxon kingdom tried to <u>pay</u> the Vikings to go away.

Why do you think the Anglo-Saxons did this?

I think they did this because they hoped the Vikings would take the money and leave them alone.

Why do you think paying the Vikings to go away never really worked?

I think it didn't work because they knew that if they came back they could get the Anglo-Saxons to pay them again.

By AD 871, Wessex was the only kingdom the Vikings hadn't defeated.

Imagine you are Alfred the Great. Write down how it feels to be the last Anglo-Saxon king standing up to the Vikings.

"I understand how the Vikings came to conquer most of England and how Alfred the Great tried to stop them."

Extension Idea

Pupils could imagine that they're an <u>advisor</u> to an Anglo-Saxon king. They should come up with <u>suggestions</u> for their king of other options of getting the Vikings to go away.

Pupils might write that they are worried the Vikings will completely take over the country. They might write that they are confident they can still beat the Vikings in battle.

The Vikings were grouped into 'ship units', so a band of warriors would be the band that crewed a particular ship. The ship would be commanded by a chieftan or an important landowner. The crew would pay themselves by taking whatever they could from the lands that they raided — and in England, they paid themselves by claiming land.

By contrast, the Anglo-Saxon fyrd was made up of men who were obliged to fight for their thegn for a certain number of days. They were not paid for their service, and could be fined if they didn't turn up for duty.

Extension Idea

Discuss this information about the 'ship units' and the fyrds. Which do pupils think would fight more fiercely, and be better disciplined — and why?

Alfred the Great

Vikings: Activity Book p.22-23

Alfred the Great really did love learning. He wrote: "He seems to me a very foolish man, and truly wretched, who will not increase his understanding while he is in the world, and ever wish and long to reach that endless life where all will be made clear."

Suggested Scaffolding:

"Try and include these words in your answer:
- *baptised*
- *retreat"*

Extension Idea

Pupils could pretend to be Guthrum. They could write diary entries describing how they felt after the first treaty with Alfred, when they had to become a Christian, and after the second treaty, when they were given the Danelaw.

22

Alfred the Great

The Viking leader Guthrum defeated Alfred the Great in battle at Chippenham. Alfred then went into <u>hiding</u> in the Somerset marshes.

Read page 22 of the Study Book.

> What do you think Alfred was doing while he was hiding out in the marshes?

I think he was preparing his army for the next battle with the Vikings.

Alfred went on to <u>defeat</u> Guthrum in the Battle of Edington. Alfred made Guthrum sign a <u>peace treaty</u>.

> In your own words, write down what Guthrum had to do as part of this peace treaty.

Guthrum had to be baptised as a Christian. He then had to leave Wessex and retreat back to East Anglia.

Page 23 of the Study Book explains how peace with Guthrum didn't last. Alfred and Guthrum had another battle. They signed another treaty, which created an area of land called the <u>Danelaw</u>.

> Colour in the area on this map covered by the Danelaw. Label it 'Danelaw'.

> Using a different colour, colour in the land controlled by Alfred. Label it 'Alfred's land'.

Danelaw

Alfred's land

Alfred the Great: National Curriculum Aims

- Know and understand the history of Britain as a chronological narrative.
- Know how people's lives have shaped Britain.
- Create structured accounts.

Read this fact file about Alfred the Great.

> Fact File: Alfred the Great.
>
> Born: AD 849
>
> Died: AD 899
>
> King of Wessex from: AD 871 to: AD 899
>
> Married to: Eahlswith
>
> Number of children: five

Historians often write biographies for important people in history.
A biography is the story of someone's life.

Write a biography of Alfred the Great. Use the information in the fact file to help you, along with the information on pages 22 to 23 of the Study Book.

Alfred the Great was born in AD 849, and became king of Wessex in AD 871. His wife was Eahlswith, and they had 5 children. He defeated the Viking leader Guthrum in battle and signed a treaty with him to create the Danelaw. Alfred also thought that learning was very important. Thanks to the Viking attacks, education in England wasn't very good, so Alfred had books made and sent them to bishops to teach from. He set up his own school, and ordered a history of the Anglo-Saxons to be written. He died in AD 899.

"I understand how Alfred the Great got his name and what he did to defeat the Vikings in England."

Pupil Guidance:

"Try to include some of the good things Alfred is remembered for doing in his life, as well as the facts in the Fact File."

Pupils should include information from <u>both</u> the Fact File and the Study Book in their answer.

Extension Idea

Alfred kept a little notebook for writing down thoughts and ideas. Ask pupils to imagine what he would have written when he had to start putting England back on its feet again. What would his priorities have been — building ships to attack the Vikings at sea, or improving schools and learning?

Pupils could write about Alfred's military successes in more detail. For example, that he <u>reorganised the army</u> and <u>built battleships</u> to fight the Vikings at sea.

The Danes and the Danelaw

Vikings: Activity Book p.24-25

Unlike most women of the time, Aethelfleda had only one child. The monks who wrote about her noted that after the painful birth, she refused to become pregnant again, and decided to devote herself to arms.

Extension Idea

Pupils could discuss which part of Mercia they'd rather live in (the Viking half or King Alfred's half) and give some reasons why.

Pupils could include other facts from the Study Book. For example, Aethelfleda fortified Mercia against the Danes and built many fortresses there.

Extension Idea

Pupils could write a similar fact file about the Danelaw.

24

The Danes and the Danelaw

By AD 886, the Vikings were in control of an area of Britain called the Danelaw.

Why do you think this area was known as the Danelaw?

I think it was known as the Danelaw because *some of the Vikings came from Denmark and were called Danes. They controlled the law in that part of the land.*

Which English kingdom was split in two when the Danelaw was made? Use the map on page 24 of the Study Book to help you. Tick the correct answer below.

Northumbria ☐   Mercia ☑   East Anglia ☐   Wessex ☐

Aethelfleda was a great warrior.
She was also an Anglo-Saxon queen who fought against the Danes.

Read the information about Aethelfleda on page 24 of the Study Book. Use it to write down four key facts about Aethelfleda.

Fact 1: *Aethelfleda was King Alfred's eldest daughter.*

Fact 2: *Aethelfleda was married to Aethelred.*

Fact 3: *Aethelfleda led the Mercian Army.*

Fact 4: *Aethelfleda took charge of the defence of English Mercia after her husband died.*

Extension Idea

Pupils could do more research on Aethelfleda, the Lady of the Mercians, and how she was different from the majority of women of her time. Pupils could write her autobiography, including reflections she might have had on her life and times.

The Danes and the Danelaw: National Curriculum Aims

- Know and understand the history of Britain as a chronological narrative.
- Understand how evidence is used to make historical claims.

Read page 25 of the Study Book.

How could a Viking get his own bit of land in the Danelaw?

Loyal warriors were rewarded with land and were allowed to throw out the original Anglo-Saxon landowners and take over the land themselves.

Extension Idea

Pupils could be asked to imagine that they are an Anglo-Saxon <u>landowner</u> who has been thrown off his land by a Viking. They could write a <u>letter</u> to a friend explaining what happened and how they feel about this.

Draw and <u>label</u> one piece of evidence that archaeologists have found which shows that Viking <u>women</u> lived in the Danelaw.

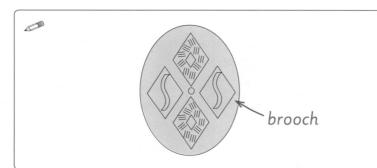

brooch

Pupils should draw one or both of the Viking woman's <u>brooches</u> found by archaeologists in Yorkshire.

In your own words, write down why an <u>Anglo-Saxon woman</u> living in the Danelaw might have agreed to <u>marry</u> a <u>Viking man</u>.

If a woman's male relatives had died, she might struggle to support herself. If she then married a Viking man, she would have some support, for example somewhere to live and food to eat.

Suggested Scaffolding:

'If a woman's male relatives had died...'

"I know about the Danelaw and how the Vikings settled there."

Viking Jorvik

Vikings: Activity Book p.26-27

26

Viking Jorvik

The Vikings ruled the Danelaw from the city of <u>Jorvik</u>, which we now know as <u>York</u>.

Read page 26 of the Study Book. Write down <u>three</u> reasons why Jorvik was the ideal place for the Vikings to settle.

Reason 1) *They could sail right up the river from the sea.*

Reason 2) *They could use the river for trade.*

Reason 3) *The rivers would have made Jorvik easy to defend.*

Archaeologists know a lot about what life was like in Viking Jorvik from excavations in a part of York called <u>Coppergate</u>.

Draw <u>one</u> object from pages 26 to 27 of the Study Book that archaeologists dug up from Coppergate. Write down <u>what it is</u> and what it's <u>made of</u>.

My drawing is of a

....

It's made of

....

What's special about the <u>soil</u> in Coppergate? How did it help the archaeologists digging there?

Hint: the answer is on page 26 of the Study Book.

The soil in Coppergate is *wet and soft.*

This helped archaeologists because *it stopped many items that were buried there from rotting away, and also meant that they could dig a long way down.*

Extension Idea

Pupils could discuss whether or not the place that <u>they live</u> would have been a <u>suitable place</u> for Vikings to settle.

Pupils might draw a Viking <u>leather boot</u>, a <u>wooden cup or bowl</u>, or a <u>comb and comb case</u> made of bone.

Extension Idea

Pupils could be asked to think about whether it's possible to find <u>everything</u> that the Vikings left behind in York. Why or why not?

Masses of animal and human dung has been found in Coppergate. Many examples of the human faeces contain eggs of parasitic worms, which would have made people sick or weak. There were no permanent remedies for this — the best you could do was take herbal teas made with a plant called wormwood, which could often make you sick.

Viking Jorvik: National Curriculum Aims

- Know and understand the history of Britain as a chronological narrative.
- Understand how evidence is used to make historical claims.
- Understand similarity and difference and use them to draw contrasts.

This photo shows what the area of Coppergate in York is like <u>today</u>.

What do you think Coppergate would have looked like in Viking times? In what ways would it have been similar to this photo? In what ways would it have been different? Use the information on page 27 of the Study Book to help you.

In Viking times, the streets would be lined with all sorts of shops, just like in the picture of Coppergate today. However, in Viking times, it wouldn't have been as spacious. Toilets, animal pens and wells would have been squeezed in between the houses, and it would probably have looked much dirtier. Buildings would have been made from wood, not brick and glass.

The Coppergate excavations told archaeologists a lot about what Vikings ate.

Imagine you are a Viking living in Coppergate. Write down what you're going to have for your meal this evening. Use page 27 of the Study Book to help you.

I am going to have beef stew with some barley bread. As a treat, I will have some fruit for my pudding.

"I know what life was like in Viking Jorvik and what evidence we have for this."

Pupil Guidance:

"What can you see in the photo? What are the people doing? What would people have been doing in Viking times? What would the buildings have looked like then?"

Pupils may give many different answers, but the best answers will make <u>direct comparisons</u> between modern-day Coppergate and Viking Coppergate.

Pupils can suggest any meal as long as it is made up of components listed on page 27 of the Study Book, or foods that would have definitely been available in Viking York.

Extension Idea

Pupils could investigate the website of the Jorvik Viking Centre and find out more about what life was like in this Viking city. They could then make a fact file about the city.

Athelstan and Constantine

Vikings: Activity Book p.28-29

Pupils could also give other facts, such as that he united England as one kingdom.

Extension Idea

Pupils could be asked to write a biography of King Athelstan based on the information on pages 28-29 of the Study Book.

More able pupils might have named the kingdom as Alba.

Extension Idea

Athelstan and Constantine both wanted to look after their countries, but they came into conflict because of this. Discuss why they found it necessary to go to war with each other. What might have happened if they had sat down together and discussed Scottish independence and English security, rather than going to war?

28

Athelstan and Constantine

Athelstan and Constantine were two important figures in British history.

Read page 28 of the Study Book. Who was King Athelstan?

King Athelstan was the grandson of King Alfred the Great, and he was King of England.

Who was King Constantine? Write down two things Constantine had done by AD 904. All the information you need is on page 28 of the Study Book.

King Constantine was king of Scotland.

By AD 904 King Constantine had forced the Vikings who were invading Scotland to retreat and he'd also started reorganising the Scottish tribes into one kingdom.

Use pages 28 to 29 of the Study Book to find out if the following sentences are true or false. Tick the correct box.

In 918, Constantine took control of the top part of Northumbria.   True ✓ False ☐

The Vikings were trapped in the middle of Constantine and Athelstan.   True ✓ False ☐

Constantine attacked Athelstan at the fortress of Dunnottar.   True ☐ False ✓

The battle between Constantine and Athelstan at Brunanburh was one of the smallest battles of the time.   True ☐ False ✓

Extension Idea

Higher ability pupils could be asked to write correct versions of the false statements.

Athelstan and Constantine: National Curriculum Aims

- Know and understand the history of Britain as a chronological narrative.
- Know how people's lives have shaped Britain.
- Understand cause and consequence.

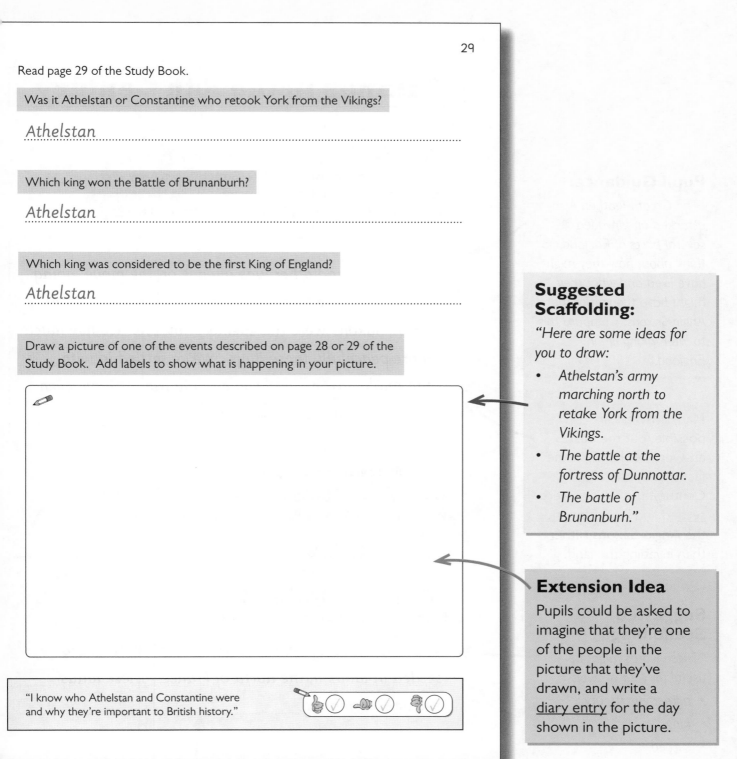

29

Read page 29 of the Study Book.

Was it Athelstan or Constantine who retook York from the Vikings?

Athelstan

Which king won the Battle of Brunanburh?

Athelstan

Which king was considered to be the first King of England?

Athelstan

Draw a picture of one of the events described on page 28 or 29 of the Study Book. Add labels to show what is happening in your picture.

"I know who Athelstan and Constantine were and why they're important to British history."

Suggested Scaffolding:

"Here are some ideas for you to draw:

- *Athelstan's army marching north to retake York from the Vikings.*
- *The battle at the fortress of Dunnottar.*
- *The battle of Brunanburh."*

Extension Idea

Pupils could be asked to imagine that they're one of the people in the picture that they've drawn, and write a <u>diary entry</u> for the day shown in the picture.

Extension Idea

Territorial disputes in this period were often settled by war, not negotiation. Has anything changed now, or do leaders in the modern day world still behave like Athelstan and Constantine?

Vikings in the 10th Century

Vikings: Activity Book p.30-31

30

Vikings in the 10th Century

Read page 30 of the Study Book.

Imagine you are a Viking living in England in the 10th Century. Your great-grandfather was part of the Great Heathen Army who attacked and invaded England from Denmark. In the box below, write about how your life is different to your great-grandfather's life.

> *My great-grandfather was always on the move, going from one battle to another and claiming land. The Anglo-Saxons were the enemy. However, we live much more peacefully these days. We've settled in with the Anglo-Saxons, and some of my friends have even married Anglo-Saxon women.*

10th Century Scandinavian Vikings were still invading places abroad.

Take another look at page 30 of the Study Book.
What city in France did the Viking Rollo try to invade in AD 911?

Paris

What happened between Rollo and the French king after this unsuccessful invasion?

Rollo made an agreement with the French king and settled in lands in the north of France. These lands became Normandy.

Pupil Guidance:

"The Great Heathen Army attacked and invaded several parts of England, so think about how they might have lived and what they might have thought of the Anglo-Saxons. Compare this to later Viking life in England."

Many answers are possible, but the best answers will highlight the fact that by the 10th Century, the Vikings were settled and living alongside the Anglo-Saxons rather than invading the land.

Suggested Scaffolding:

"These words might be useful for your answer:
- *agreement/treaty*
- *king*
- *settled*
- *Normandy"*

Higher ability pupils might write about the duchy of Normandy.

Vikings in the 10th Century: National Curriculum Aims
- Create structured accounts.
- Understand similarity and difference and use them to draw contrasts.
- Know about the history of the wider world.
- Understand the connections between religious and social history.

31

Olaf Trygvasson and Harold Bluetooth were both Viking kings who converted to Christianity. They both tried to force the people they ruled to become Christian too. Read page 31 of the Study Book.

What country was Harold Bluetooth king of?

Denmark

Do you think it's <u>fair</u> for a king to make all the people in his kingdom follow the same religion as him? Why or why not?

....

....

....

This photo shows a Viking metal-smith's mould, which was found in Denmark.

The metal-smith could use the mould to make <u>Christian crosses</u> and <u>Thor's hammers</u> (a <u>Pagan symbol</u>) for his customers.

Why do you think a Viking metal-smith might have had a mould that could make both crosses and Pagan symbols?

The metal-smith might have lived in a place where people followed different religions. He could then make a cross or a hammer depending on what his customer wanted.

"I know what life was like for 10th Century Vikings both in England and abroad."

Extension Idea

Pupils could design a <u>leaflet</u> for Harold Bluetooth to send to all of his people, trying to <u>persuade</u> them to <u>become Christians</u>.

Pupils can give either answer here, as long as they back it up with a good <u>reason</u>.

Pupil Guidance:

"Some people converted to Christianity when their king wanted them to. But some people kept their Pagan religion."

Since the Vikings already believed in several gods, some of them might have continued to worship <u>Pagan gods</u> like Thor while practising <u>Christianity</u>.

Aethelred is Unready!

Vikings: Activity Book p.32-33

32

Aethelred is Unready!

King Aethelred is definitely not one of England's best loved kings.
He had a bit of an unfortunate nickname as a result.

Read page 32 of the Study Book. How did Aethelred the
Unready get his nickname? Tick the correct box below.

☐ *He was called 'Unready' because he
never got dressed in the morning.*

☐ *He was called 'Unready', which means 'always late'
because he was always late to meetings with his advisors.*

☑ *He was called 'Unready', which means 'bad advice'
because he received bad advice from his advisors.*

Aethelred the Unready became king in AD 978.
A second wave of Viking raids on England started in AD 980.

Why did the Vikings come back again and again after these raids?
Use page 32 of the Study Book to help you.

*It became clear to the Vikings that Aethelred didn't have
the power or the organisation to defend England against
their raids.*

Read page 33 of the Study Book.

Aethelred repeatedly paid the Vikings money to go away.
What was this money called?

Danegeld

Extension Idea

Pupils could choose
another king from the
Study Book and make up
a <u>nickname</u> for him, along
with a reason for it.

Pupil Guidance:

*"What made it easy for the
Vikings to keep attacking?"*

Extension Idea

Pupils could be asked for
suggestions of what the
Vikings did with the
<u>money</u> that the
Anglo-Saxons gave them.

Between 980 and 991, the Danes were helped by their cousins in Normandy. Richard of Normandy,
grandson of the Rollo we met on the last page, was allowing Danish raiders to use Norman
harbours. This caused so much trouble between the Normans and the English that the Pope in
Rome intervened to make peace, and ensure that the Normans did not help the Danish Vikings.

Aethelred is Unready: National Curriculum Aims
- Know and understand the history of Britain as a chronological narrative.
- Create structured accounts.
- Know how people's lives have shaped Britain.

33

Today's <u>newspapers</u> have articles about things the government is doing. If the Anglo-Saxons had had newspapers, what sort of things might they have said about Aethelred?

Imagine you work for an Anglo-Saxon newspaper. Write an <u>article</u> about <u>Aethelred</u>, what he is doing to <u>stop</u> the Vikings, and why it <u>won't work</u>!

Use page 33 of the Study Book to help you.

Aethelred, the King of England, is playing a dangerous game with the Vikings. Each time they come to attack and raid our lands, Aethelred gives in to their demands, and hands over England's money to pay them to go away. He's not only done this once — he keeps doing it, and they keep coming back. They know that Aethelred will keep handing over the silver, so they're just going to keep on coming.

In AD 1002, Aethelred ordered <u>all</u> the <u>Danish men</u> in England to be <u>killed</u>. This was called the <u>St Brice's Day Massacre</u>.

Do you think it was <u>fair</u> of Aethelred to make this order? Why or why not?

....

....

....

....

"I know how Aethelred the Unready got his nickname and how he failed to stop Viking attacks on England."

Suggested Scaffolding:
- 'Aethelred keeps paying the Vikings to...'
- 'This is a bad idea because...'

Pupils might write a variety of different articles here but they must cover both parts of the question.

Extension Idea
Pupils could imagine that they are <u>King Aethelred</u> and that they have read this newspaper article. They could write King Aethelred's <u>response</u> to reading it.

Pupils might answer either way for this question, but any answer that is supported with an appropriate reason is fine.

Extension Idea
Aethelred wasn't the first or the last king to be considered unsuitable for the job, either because they were unwise, cruel, corrupt or ineffective. What options existed for the English at this time if they didn't like their king? Investigate and discuss.

King Canute and Emma

Vikings: Activity Book p.34-35

Canute was a strong and able king. He reformed the law, and made it fairer to ordinary people, and he improved the coinage, making English coins equal in weight to Scandinavian ones. He was respected abroad as well — when the new Holy Roman Emperor was crowned in Rome, Canute was invited.

Extension Idea

Higher ability pupils could write a set of mixed-up sentences about another event in history using the Study Book for help. They could then swap with a partner and find the correct order.

Pupils might answer this question in a variety of ways, but the answer must be linked to the events in England at the time.

Pupil Guidance:

"What was happening in England that Aethelred was running away from?"

34

King Canute and Emma

The St. Brice's Day Massacre caused anger amongst the Vikings.

Number the sentences below from 1 to 7 to show the order of events after the St. Brice's Day Massacre. The first and last events have been numbered for you.

Page 34 of the Study Book will help you.

3	King Aethelred runs away to Normandy.
6	Aethelred dies, and his son Edmund becomes King.
1	King Sweyn Forkbeard of Norway invades England.
7	Edmund dies, and Canute becomes King of England.
5	Aethelred comes back from Normandy to be King.
2	England fights against the Vikings, raising money to pay them off.
4	Sweyn becomes King of England, but dies a few weeks later.

Imagine that you're King Aethelred, and that you've just fled from England to Normandy. Write a letter to a friend to explain why you've run away.

Dear friend,

I've arrived in Normandy after escaping from England. It was becoming impossible to stay. The Vikings kept raiding over and over again, and my country was getting poorer and poorer. I just knew I couldn't beat the Vikings and make them go away for good, so I've had to flee. I didn't know what else to do.

Extension Idea

Pupils could write a reply back to King Aethelred, giving him advice about what he should do.

King Canute and Emma: National Curriculum Aims

- Know and understand the history of Britain as a chronological narrative.
- Create structured accounts.
- Understand change.

King Aethelred's second wife was called <u>Emma</u>. After Aethelred had died, she <u>married Canute</u>. This helped the English people to accept him as their king.

Write down <u>two</u> other things Canute did during his reign that helped him to be liked by people in England. Use page 34 of the Study Book to help you.

1) *Canute stopped the Vikings raiding.*

2) *He made sure that Britain was involved in international trade.*

Imagine you were living in England when Canute was king. How would you have felt about having a <u>Viking</u> for a king? Why?

I would have felt

because

Have a look at the <u>family tree</u> on page 35 of the Study Book.

How was <u>Emma</u> related to the Duke of Normandy?

She was his daughter. / He was her father.

After <u>Canute's</u> death, who do you think took over his role as King of Denmark?

Harthacnut

"I know about King Canute's reign in England."

Extension Idea
Pupils could be asked to consider how <u>Emma felt</u> about marrying a Viking and why she might have agreed to do so.

Pupils might also say that Canute used the English people to conquer most of Scandinavia.

Pupils could answer this in several ways, but any answer that is supported with an appropriate reason is fine.

Pupil Guidance:
"The box under Emma and Canute on the family tree shows their children. What do you think the <u>crown symbol</u> means?"

Extension Idea
How might our lives have been different if we had curtinued to be ruled by Danish kings, and become part of a Scandinavian empire? Would it make a difference to how we live today? Pupils could find out more about the countries of Norway, Sweden and Denmark before they answer.

The Kings After Canute

Vikings: Activity Book p.36-37

The Kings After Canute

When King Canute died, there was a lot of <u>fighting</u> over who should take the throne.

There were <u>four options</u> for the next <u>King of England</u> after Canute. Read page 36 of the Study Book. Who were the four options? Complete the sentences below.

The options were __Edward__ and

__Alfred__ (Queen Emma's sons by Aethelred),

__Harold Harefoot__ (King Canute's son by his first wife),

and __Harthacnut__ (Emma and Canute's son).

<u>Edward</u> was eventually crowned King of England, but the throne didn't pass straight from Canute to him. Complete the timeline below to show how the crown passed to Edward.

Page 36 of the Study Book will help you with this.

1035 — King Canute dies.

1037 — __Harold__, who is looking after the throne for Harthacnut, takes the crown for himself.

__1040__ — Harthacnut takes back his throne.

1042 — Harthacnut dies and offers the throne to __Edward__.

Queen Emma's son <u>Alfred</u> met an unhappy end. In your own words, write down what happened to him. Use page 36 of the Study Book for help.

Alfred was captured by Godwine, the Earl of Wessex.
Alfred was blinded and died from his wounds.

Suggested Scaffolding:

"You'll need these names for your answer:
- *Alfred*
- *Edward*
- *Harthacnut*
- *Harold Harefoot"*

Pupils might also write that Edward, Alfred's brother, held Godwine <u>responsible</u> for his <u>brother's death</u>.

Extension Idea

Ask pupils to find out more about the first five sons of Earl Godwine: Sweyn, Tostig, Harold, Gyrth and Leofwine. Discuss why they became so powerful.

The Kings After Canute: National Curriculum Aims

• Know and understand the history of Britain as a chronological narrative.
• Create structured accounts.
• Understand change.
• Understand the connections between political and social history.

King Edward had to rely on his <u>earls</u> for support.

> Read page 37 of the Study Book. Write down <u>one</u> thing that the king needed his earls to do.

He needed them to collect together the men for the fyrd / army.

Edward had particular problems with one earl, called <u>Godwine</u>.

> Imagine you are King Edward. It's AD 1052. Write a letter to your mother telling her about the problems you are having with Godwine and your other earls.

> *Dear Mother,*
> Do you remember that troublesome Earl Godwine?
> I sent him away last year, but now he and his sons
> are back with an army and it looks like I'm going to
> have to let him stay. If only I had the support of my
> other earls! But he is their friend and they won't help
> me get rid of him. It's just not fair.

> How do you think the <u>ordinary people</u> in England felt whilst the fighting over Canute's throne was happening?

I think they felt bored of the arguing. They couldn't decide who would be the next king, and they had to focus on supporting their family and making sure they had enough to eat.

> "I know about what happened to the throne in England after Canute died."

Pupils might also write that these were armed men, whom the earls collected from their <u>estates</u>.

Extension Idea
Pupils could be asked to imagine that they are King Edward and write <u>how they feel</u> about having to <u>rely on a fyrd</u> to fight for their country in the case of an invasion.

Pupil Guidance:
"Remember, Godwine was exiled in AD 1051. What happened after that?"

Extension Idea
Pupils could imagine that they are <u>Edward's mother</u> and write a <u>response</u> telling Edward what he should do.

Pupils could answer this in several ways. They might also write that the people could have felt angry about not having a say in who would be king.

The Conqueror is Coming

Vikings: Activity Book p.38-39

The Conqueror is Coming

After he died, the Christian Church declared that <u>King Edward</u> was a <u>saint</u>.
A saint is somebody the church thinks is very religious or holy.
Read page 38 of the Study Book.

Why do you think Edward was made a saint?

I think Edward was made a saint because he lived a very religious life. He gave money to the church and supported monks, as well as going to church regularly.

What nickname is King Edward known by? Circle the correct answer below.

Edward the Conqueror   (Edward the Confessor)   Edward the Professor

Edward spent most of his childhood in <u>Normandy</u>.

Where is Normandy?

Normandy is in France

King Edward didn't have any children, so he had no son to pass the throne on to when he died. Several people wanted it though...

Which <u>three</u> people wanted the throne when King Edward died?
Use page 39 of the Study Book to help you.

1) Harold Godwineson
2) William, the Duke of Normandy
3) Harald Hardrada

Pupils might also write that he followed <u>church rules</u> or that England was <u>peaceful</u> under his rule.

Extension Idea

Pupils could be asked to look for Normandy on a <u>map of France</u>.

Extension Idea

Pupils could do a <u>role-play</u>, where they pretend to be the people wanting the crown and put across their <u>arguments</u> about why they should be king.

William of Normandy was the son of Robert of Normandy, and his mistress, Herleva. At that time, being born out of wedlock was regarded as shameful and such children were termed 'bastards'. Many thought he should not have succeeded his father.

The Conqueror is Coming: National Curriculum Aims

- Know and understand the history of Britain as a chronological narrative.
- Understand change.
- Understand cause and consequence.

Just like when King Canute died, when King Edward died, people fought over the right to his throne. This led to several battles.

Who was crowned King of England after King Edward's death?

Harold Godwineson .... was crowned King of England.

In the box below, write a list of the events that happened from when the new King of England was <u>crowned</u> to the end of the <u>Battle of Hastings</u>.

Page 39 of the Study Book will help you with this.

- _William was angry that Harold had been crowned and began building ships to invade Britain._
- _Harald Hardrada invaded, and King Harold fought him at Stamford Bridge. Harald Hardrada was killed._
- _William then invaded, and King Harold fought him at the Battle of Hastings. Harold was killed._

How might the events of 1066 have been different if Edward had <u>had a son</u>?

The throne would have passed straight to Edward's son. This would have avoided all of the fighting, and William the Conqueror wouldn't have become king.

"I know how William of Normandy became King of England."

Suggested Scaffolding:

- 'William began building...'
- 'Harald Hardrada invaded...'
- 'William then invaded...'

Extension Idea

Pupils could research the <u>Battle of Hastings</u> using books or the internet. They could try to find out what <u>date</u> it took place and <u>where</u>, and <u>how</u> William defeated Harold.

Pupil Guidance:

"Think about who would have become king if Edward had had a son."

Pupils may write that there might still have been fighting if people didn't think that Edward's son was suitable.

Extension Idea

Pupils could find out more about the Bayeux Tapestry, research the life of William of Normandy, and then draw a Bayeux Tapestry of their own, showing the details of his life and what happened to him.

Picture acknowledgements

AS/A LEVEL YEAR 1

WORKBOOK

FOR THE NEW
2015
SPECIFICATIONS

Biology

Organisms exchange substances with
their environment • Genetic information,
variation and relationships between organisms

Pauline Lowrie

PHILIP ALLAN FOR
HODDER
EDUCATION
LEARN MORE

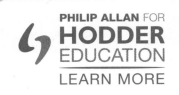

WORKBOOK

Contents

① **This workbook will help you** to prepare for your AQA AS/A-level biology exam.

② **Your exam** is 1 hour 30 minutes long for each of two AS papers, and 2 hours long for each of three A-level papers.

③ **For each topic** there are:
- stimulus materials, including key terms and concepts
- short-answer questions that build up to exam-style questions
- spaces for you to write or plan your answers
- questions that test your mathematical skills

④ **Answering the questions** will help you to build your skills and meet the assessment objectives AO1 (knowledge and understanding), AO2 (application) and AO3 (analysis).

⑤ **You still need to** read your textbook and refer to your revision guides and lesson notes.

⑥ **Marks** available are provided for all the questions so that you can gauge the level of detail needed in your answers.

⑦ **Timings** are given for the exam-style questions to make your practice as realistic as possible.

⑧ **Answers** are available at:
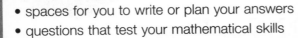
www.hoddereducation.co.uk/workbookanswers